Containers.
Terrariums • Mini Greenhouses • Terra Cotta Pots • Baby Food Jars • Glass Vases • Glass Bottles • Plastic Saucers • Plastic Pot Liners

Don't limit yourself to the containers listed… anything that holds water has the potential to become a creative indoor gardening vessel! Craft stores have huge sections of unique glassware, bottles and terra cotta pieces.

Filler. Potting Soil • Charcoal • Perlite • Vermiculite
Decorative Filler: Marbles • Gems • Rocks • Gravel

Plants.
Seeds • Bulbs • Herbs • Greenery • Flowering Plants • Aquatic Plants

Layered Soil
Many projects will refer to layering soil. Layering gives a fun visual effect as well as being nutritious for plants. Unless otherwise directed, use this basic ratio when layering soil:
Top - 3 parts potting soil
Middle - 2 parts other filler - perlite, vermiculite or moss
Bottom - 1 part charcoal - for soil freshness and drainage

MW00826234

Small Terrariums

Virtually any watertight glass jar or bottle can become a mini greenhouse. Terrariums are miniature versions of full-sized greenhouses complete with glass panes. A green thumb is not required, because they recycle moisture. Terrariums can often go a month or more between waterings.

MATERIALS: Terrarium • Soil mixture • Gravel, rocks or marbles • Charcoal • Perlite or vermiculite • Green or flowering plant • Sponge on a skewer

PLANTS: Baby's Tears* ^ • Creeping Fig* ^ • Wandering Jew* • Many Varieties of Ferns • African Violets • Dwarf Begonias • Orchids • Pitcher Plant • Sundew • Venus Fly-trap • Boxwood • Mosses

*Aggressive grower
^Better for shallow gardens

INSTRUCTIONS:

Place ½" to 1" layer of gravel, rocks or marbles on bottom of terrarium for drainage.

Add a ½" layer of charcoal granules to keep soil fresh.

Add potting soil using a ratio of one part charcoal to 4 parts soil mix.

For extra color and texture, add perlite or vermiculite. Like charcoal, perlite helps with drainage, but is white, creating a stark contrast to the color of the soil. Vermiculite helps nourish the soil. Mix vermiculite with the potting soil for a supreme soil mixture or layer it for a fun visual effect. All soils combined should fill one fourth to one half of the terrarium.

Before planting, shake excess soil off the plant roots. Spoon a hole in soil. Add plant and pack soil around plant base.

Mist plant and soil. Sponge inside of terrarium to remove dirt or residue.

1. Layer the soil in container.

2. Add the plants.

3. Add the miniature garden accessories in the container.

Plant Care Tips

❀ Your plant will appreciate infrequent air circulation. If humidity builds up, leave the top open for a day. Once the foliage is dry, close the top.

❀ Sponge down the inside occasionally to eliminate dirt or bacterial growth on the glass.

❀ Indirect light is best for terrariums. Avoid direct sunlight.

❀ Do not overcrowd when planting. Avoid root contact with glass; rotting will occur.

❀ Neglect it! Overwatering is death to terrariums. To avoid the overwatering urge, use a spray bottle to mist instead of pouring water. Closed terrariums should only need water every few weeks when soil becomes dry to the touch.

Some terrariums are decorative and open from the side, but you can still use them. Plant in a small glass bowl, place the bowl inside the terrarium and surround with decorative marbles or rocks.

Terrariums with open tops make dramatic candleholders.

1. Fill bowl with dirt and add plant.

2. Place the bowl in the terrarium and add the stones.

1. Open the terrarium and arrange the candles inside.

2. Add the glass marbles.

3. Embellish with greenery.

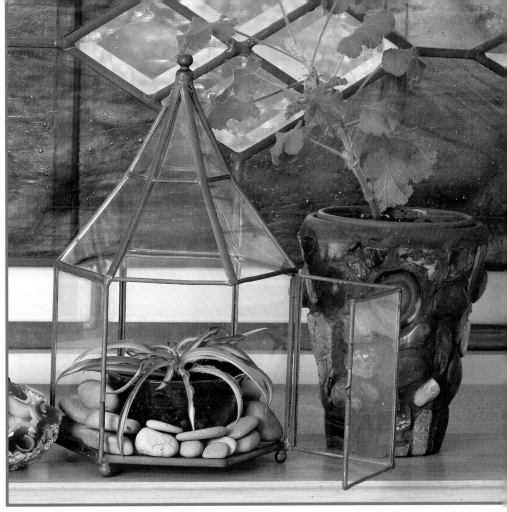

Beautiful Glass Gardens & Terrariums

If a terrarium seems too exotic for your taste, simplify the look of your garden using a piece of glassware. If it's clear and watertight, it can be turned into a glass garden. Select your container, then get crafty and add garden motif miniatures for a charming scene. Follow the same instructions for building a terrarium, but leave some space on the soil surface for adding miniatures.

INSTRUCTIONS: Follow Terrarium instructions on page 4 leaving room to add garden miniature accessories.

Jars with Lid
These jars from Provo Craft are made specifically for gardens. The wide base is perfect for adding miniatures and creating a charming garden scene.

Baby Food Jar
Make a mini garden using a baby food jar. This is a perfect gift making project for a child.

Garden Accessory Tips

❀ Add miniatures to your terrarium that echo the decor of the room.

❀ Make a miniature Japanese garden. Arrange small tree like plants, a few stones and rake the soil in decorative patterns.

❀ Using three to five small terrariums, make a continuing scene with garden miniatures.

❀ For a wedding gift, make a scene with a bride and groom standing in front of a church. Or a christening or baptism gift with a church and happy family complete with a tiny baby.

❀ Welcome a new neighbor with a terrarium filled with special greenery accented with tiny balloons and a welcome sign.

1. Arrange silk petals around edge of cake plate.

2. Add soil, plants and miniature accessories to plastic container.

3. Position lid over plastic container.

Bubble Bowl on Candlestick Holder

Plant garden in 8" bubble bowl and place on any glass candlestick holder. Seal with a 6" mirror.

Cake Stand Garden

Use 8" plastic plant liner. Place on cake pedestal. Scatter silk rose petals, potpourri or marbles around liner. Seal with cover.

These creative gardens are easy to make and easy to care for!

Seed Crafting Tips

Growing plants from seeds is a craft many of you tried back in elementary school. You decorated a paper cup and added some soil and sunflower seeds. It sat in the classroom window and was watered daily until a sprout appeared. You proudly brought it home as a present for mom or dad. Now you can upscale this basic craft into a unique gift.

Indoor Seed Basics

❀ Seeds germinating indoors need about 16 hours of light and a dark period at night.

❀ Direct window light is beneficial but fluorescent lighting is helpful to seedlings.

❀ Keep seedlings moist but not soggy at all times.

❀ Normal indoor temperatures, 68 to 78°F, are ideal for germination. A drop in temperature at night is fine.

❀ If you plan to replant your seedlings outside, introduce them to the yard slowly, a few hours at a time. In about a week, the plants are ready to be outside.

❀ Your seed packet may have other instructions specific to that plant variety. Remember to look inside the packet for detailed information.

Garden in a Jar

Seed Packet Decoupage Pot

MATERIALS: Terra Cotta Clay pot • Foam brush • Mod Podge • Seed packets • Light Blue acrylic paint • Raffia

1. Apply Mod Podge to pot.

2. Add the seed packets.

3. Paint rim. Tie a raffia bow.

Garden in a Jar

MATERIALS: Mason jar • Layered soil mixture, see page 2 for recipe • Seeds • Ribbon • 6" to 7" square of fabric

INSTRUCTIONS: Pour each soil layer into jar, gently shaking to settle layers evenly. Start with ¾" of charcoal and add same amount of perlite then vermiculite. Fill the rest of the jar with potting soil leaving ½" at the top to plant seeds. Plant the seeds.

Place fabric square on top of sealed jar and tie with ribbon. Cut fabric or rip it for a fringed look or round corners with scissors for a fabric circle. Add the seed packet to ribbon tie as decoration, gluing a piece of cardstock with basic seed care instructions on back.

Water sparingly, 2 tablespoons at a time. You can replace lid and set jar on a bright window sill to create a greenhouse effect. Once sprouts appear, leave lid off and care for plants as you would any other plant. If the jar is a gift, be sure to let recipient know seedlings should be transplanted into a garden when they have grown taller.

VARIATION: Fill entire jar with soil layers, but do not plant seeds. Fill in reverse order with soil on bottom and charcoal on top so that when poured into a pot, soil is in the correct planting order. Your gift recipient can then plant seeds in their own pot.

1. Layer the soil and filler in the jar with soil first.

2. Add the lid, fabric and bow to give as a gift..

3. Your gift recipient can pour the jar contents into a pot.

4. Plant seeds and watch them grow.

Cat Grass Treat - Give the cat lover in your life something for Fluffy! Cat grass is a healthy, yummy kitty treat.

Healthy Juicer - The health nut you know will appreciate his or her own personal wheat grass garden. Wheat grass is all the rage for healthy drinks. Just grow and juice it!

Flowers for Grandma - Nothing says love like flowers. Have your child plant and decorate a special jar for Grandma. Use wildflower mixes, daisies or impatiens in a mason jar.

For the Cook - Plant herbs, oregano, parsley or rosemary for a kitchen windowsill treat.

other gift ideas!

Beautiful Bulbs

You don't have to have a well-tended garden in your yard to have beautiful flowers in bloom. Take the fragrant beauty of fresh living flowers indoors by forcing bulbs. The term forcing means growing indoors and making plants bloom before their normal season.

Bulbs have everything inside them to make them grow. They only need water and warmth to begin the process. Most bulbs are planted from September to November when temperatures are cool. The dawn of spring wakes them from hibernation and they begin to grow. In order to force bulbs, you need to trick them into thinking it is spring. Play Mother Nature!

Bulb Shapes & Sizes

1½" Hyacinth   2½" Daffodil or Narcissus   1½" Tulip

Cooling the Bulbs

Some high end nurseries and craft stores sell pre-cooled bulbs. This means you take them home and plant them! No other step is necessary.

If your bulbs are not precooled, follow these easy steps: Place bulbs in a brown paper bag, fold to close and place in the refrigerator for 4 to 15 weeks depending on the variety. Do not store near fruits, especially apples, as they emit ethylene gas that will prevent your bulbs from flowering. Label the bag so that family members do not mistake your bulbs for a salad topping! When placed in water, the cooled bulbs will grow at room temperature. Roots and green shoots will emerge immediately and you'll have flowers in 2 to 6 weeks, depending on the variety.

Bulb Flowers

Many popular flowers start as bulbs. Iris, Tulips, Narcissus, Crocus, Hyacinths and Amaryllis are just a short list of bulbs to force and each has many varieties that yield different flower shapes and colors. The most popular forcing bulbs are listed below.

Tulip - A traditional spring flower, tulips come in almost all colors except blue. You can also grow striking multi-colored varieties. Bulbs are about 1½" tall and they are onion shaped.

Hyacinth - Hyacinths muscari is known as a grape hyacinth. It produces blue tones and grassy foliage. Hyacinths orientalis yields red, white, pink, yellow, blue or purple bell-shaped flowers. Bulbs are about 1½" tall and walnut shaped.

Narcissus - More commonly known as a daffodil, these bulbs come in many beautiful varieties. Paper Whites, narcissus tazetta, are the most popular. Bridal Crowns boast double blossoms while King Alfreds have large yellow trumpet-shaped flowers. Bulbs are larger, about 2½" tall, and avocado-shaped.

1. Add the rocks, marbles or gravel to container.

2. Place the bulb on top.

3. Allow bulb to sprout.

BASIC INSTRUCTIONS: In a shallow glass bowl, place 1" to 2" of rocks, marbles, or gravel. Gently press onion shaped bulbs, wide end down and pointed end up, into rocks. Add water to cover bulbs halfway. Water daily, maintaining water level. In days you'll have roots, in a week you'll have green stalks and in six weeks you'll have beautiful flowers!

Star Staking

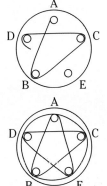

Connect the stakes in alphabetical order, winding twine around each stake and then around perimeter in a circle.

Good Tips for Bulbs

❀ Star Staking - Taller flowers like narcissus can become top heavy and start to tip over when fully bloomed. As they grow use the star staking technique (shown at left) used by professionals to keep blooms upright. Use twine or raffia and wooden dowels or skewers.

❀ Bigger is better. Bigger bulbs yield bigger flowers. Choose high grade bulbs. They may cost a little more, but are usually still under a dollar per bulb.

❀ Your container should be twice as deep as the bulb is tall.

❀ Peak bulb time for nurseries is Labor Day for the best deals and selection.

❀ Bulbs need lots of water. Water every day to maintain water level.

❀ If forcing for a special occasion, count backward from desired date. If you want a Paper White arrangement in full bloom at Christmas time, force around Thanksgiving.

Lovely Stacked Gardens

Some of the most dramatic centerpieces are the ones where height and dimension are used. Achieving this look is very easy using the simple garden crafting techniques shown here.

Tiered Bulbs

MATERIALS: 6" and 12" pedestal or footed style glass containers • Drinking glass • Rocks or marbles • Bulbs • Water

INSTRUCTIONS: Place the small glass container in the center of the large glass container. Add marbles in both containers as shown. Add bulbs to containers by slightly pressing them into marbles. Add just enough water to cover bases of bulbs. Display near light source and turn arrangement as plants start to bloom so they grow upright.

Bubble Bowl Garden

MATERIALS: 8" bubble bowl • 100 ounce brandy glass • 6" glass dish garden • 4", 6" and 8" round mirrors • Soil mix • Green ferns

INSTRUCTIONS: Fill each container with 1 part charcoal and 4 parts potting soil. Plant ferns. Stack as follows: 8" mirror, brandy glass, 6" mirror, bubble bowl, 4" mirror. Top with the dish garden. Keep the gardens moist and watch them grow!

1. Place one glass container inside the other.

2. Add glass marbles in both containers.

3. Place the flower bulbs in the containers.

4. Add water to both of the containers.

1. Place the charcoal and soil in the container.

2. Plant the fern.

3. Clean glass with a sponge on a skewer.

4. Place the mirror on top of the container.

5. Stack the bowls with plants on tops of mirrors.

Fabulous Herb Ideas

Cuisine without herbs is like a wrapped gift without a bow! Fresh herbs and herb flavored oils or vinegars add the zip and zing to even the most ordinary dish. Store-bought dried herbs can be expensive and lack the true flavor that fresh herbs boast. It's so easy to grow your own mini herb garden right on your kitchen window sill and have abundant herbs for cooking or infusing in bottles for a great gift!

1. Place herbs in bowl and crush with spoon.

Herb Gardens

You can plant your garden from seeds, see page 8, or buy small plants at a local nursery.

MATERIALS: Ceramic or glass dish garden, muffin tin or egg crate • Potting soil • Herb seeds or plants • Popsicle sticks • Paint pen • Craft glue

INSTRUCTIONS: Fill container with potting soil. Add seeds or plants (remove plants from original container and shake off dirt exposing just the roots before planting).

Using just your finger, smear a thin layer of glue on half of each popsicle stick to seal wood. Let dry for 30 minutes then write the herb name with a paint pen. The glue seal prevents paint from bleeding into wood. Stake into your garden to identify each herb.

2. Add oil or vinegar.

1. Write herb names on sticks.

2. Insert sticks in plant pots.

HERB CARE: Mist plant to remove the dirt from the leaves. Water only when the plant is dry. Keep the pot on a window sill or somewhere with sunlight. Remove herb signs before misting.

3. Seal bottle with a cork.

4. Shake vigorously to mix. Cure in a sunny place for a week or so.

5. Pour through a strainer.

Herbs & Uses

Oregano - Greek and Mexican salads
Parsley - great garnish
Mint - tea and ice cream garnish
Cilantro - salsas, soups
Rosemary - meat
Thyme - garlic spread
Basil - Italian cuisine

Create fabulous flavors for yourself or for gifts with bottles of homemade herb oils or vinegars. Use these basic instructions to get creative with your own flavor combinations. Extra Virgin Olive Oil is the best choice when infusing oil. White wine vinegar is the key to great infused vinegars. Use within 3 months for best flavor. You can also place in your kitchen for an attractive countertop accent. Your choice of bottle and finishing touches of ribbon, wire, beads and tags makes this crafty gift uniquely yours.

Infused Oils & Vinegars

MATERIALS: Airtight jar • Decorative bottle • Olive Oil or White Wine Vinegar • Claw or tweezers • Funnel • Spoon or meat tenderizer • Mini strainer • Ribbon, wire, beads, tags

INSTRUCTIONS: Crush herb sprigs or leaves with a spoon or side of a meat tenderizer. Place in airtight jar using claw, tweezers or funnel. Use ratio of 5 teaspoons of loose leaf herbs or 3 fresh sprigs to half pint of liquid. Measure oil or vinegar into bottle, pouring carefully. Seal tightly to avoid leakage when shaken or evaporation in sunlight. Shake bottle to mix and place in a sunny location for a week or two to activate infusion. Shake and taste every few days to check progress. Pour liquid through strainer into container to eliminate chunks. Pour through funnel into decorative bottle. Add fresh sprigs of herbs to bottle using a claw or tweezers. Finish with ribbon, wire or beads and add tag to identify the type of oil or vinegar.

Flavor Combinations

Garlic & Thyme Oil - A great condiment with fresh sourdough bread! Use crushed garlic, pepper, salt and fresh thyme. Accent finished bottle with thyme sprig.

Chili Oil - A must in Asian cooking. Use red pepper flakes, ginger and garlic. Bring to a boil over low heat and let cool before adding to bottle. Garnish bottle with a few chili peppers.

Chive Vinegar - Great for salad dressings or marinades. Use chive flowers to make vinegar and accent finished bottle.

Rosemary Garlic Olive Oil - Perfect for a roast rub or in sauteed pork dishes. Use crushed garlic and fresh rosemary sprigs.

More Tips

❀ Create an infused oil and vinegar combination!
❀ Add one drop of red food coloring to white wine vinegar to create color contrast in the bottle.

Soothing Aquatic Gardens

Soil isn't always necessary when working with plants. 'Indoor ponds' are attractive and elegant home accents.

Aquatic plants can be found at nurseries, but if your local garden center lacks variety, try searching online for water plants or pond plants. You can also find some water plants at pet stores that sell fish and aquarium supplies.

Plants that float are the key to an attractive water garden. Use Water Hyacinth which has long trailing roots and floating foliage clusters with spikes of pale lavender flowers or Water Lettuce that has velvety blue-green leaves forming a rosette of foliage similar to leaf lettuce.

Other plants that create dramatic underwater presentations are swimmers like Tiger Lotus, Foxtail, Anubias, Lace Plant, Sword Plant and Java Fern. Or use swimmers that ascend the surface like Sweet Flag, Umbrella Palm, Pennywort, Parrot's Feather and Bamboo Plant.

Beta Fish Environment

MATERIALS: Glass vase (ginger jar or urn shape works best) • Rocks, marbles, or gems • Plastic plant liner (size should be about diameter of vase neck) • Plastic tubing • Spathaphylum plant • Room temperature clean drinking water • Beta Fish • Beta Fish food • Chlorine removal tablets • Scissors or X-Acto knife

INSTRUCTIONS: Thoroughly clean rocks, marbles or gems and glass vase. Do not use soap. Stains may be removed with salt. Rinse well. You should be able to squeak your fingers as you rub glass. Add rocks, marbles or gems carefully. Add water, filling the vase to neck. Treat with chlorine removal tablets following manufacturer's instructions. Set aside for 2 hours until water reaches room temperature. Add fish.

Remove plant from container, shake off soil. Wash away dirt with clean drinking water. Cut hole in plant liner large enough for roots. Place plant and liner in vase, making sure roots are submerged in water but plant and liner are not. Add or subtract water if needed.

Cut about 6" of plastic tubing and place in center of plant so that it is through liner and end is 2" above water. This allows the fresh air circulation necessary for fish survival. You can also feed the fish through this tube. Add a few rocks or marbles to the base of the plant to complete garden.

Be sure that you change the water weekly. The new water should be the same temperature as the old so as not to shock the fish. Keep out of direct sunlight and at room temperature or about 72°F. Enjoy your pet!

1. Fill your container with water.

2. Treat the water to remove chlorine.

3. Add rocks and marbles to container.

4. Cut hole in the bottom of the liner.

5. Wash dirt off plant roots, insert in liner.

6. Place the liner on top of the container.

7. Insert the plastic tube in liner.

1. Place the rocks in a clean bowl.

2. Fill the container halfway with water.

3. Anchor the plant roots underwater.

Water Gardens

MATERIALS: Rocks or gravel • Glassware of any size or shape • Aquatic garden fertilizer tablets • Aquatic plants
INSTRUCTIONS: Clean glass and rocks thoroughly. Use clean filtered drinking water. When planting submerged plants, fill container halfway so gravel is submerged and you can anchor roots underwater. Use larger stones to anchor plants to the bottom if needed. Fill container rest of the way with water. Add plants. Make sure crowns of floating plants are above water.

Other Good Tips

❀ Water gardens need about 12 hours of light daily. Avoid direct sunlight as it can heat the water and burn the foliage. Fluorescent light is best.

❀ A water garden is a mini-ecosystem which will establish itself in about 3 weeks. Two weeks after set up, the water may turn cloudy with algae. In another week, the water will clear up. The aquatic plants keep the algae under control by reducing the sunlight entering the water and competing with the algae for the nutrients dissolved in the water. If algae persists, you can buy an algae corrector at your local nursery. You can also simply change the water if algae forms or if the water is looking murky and old.

❀ Add fertilizer tablets to keep plants healthy and growing.

'Lucky' Bamboo

Bamboo is the perfect plant for an indoor garden. It requires little light and no soil... and can be placed on any table. Just anchor the stalks in marbles or stones in a decorative container.

In China, bamboo is considered to be a symbol of good luck. It is often given as a gift at the 'New Year' season.

Gifts of bamboo are given at times of celebration to wish good fortune.

3 stalks attract happiness

5 stalks attract wealth

7 stalks result in good health

21 stalks give a powerful, all purpose blessing

Bamboo - Use rocks or marbles and plant bamboo in a glass container. Freshen the inch or two of water every 15 days.